D1134180

Series 708
Lives of the Great Scientists

'*Lives of the Great Scientists*'

Madame CURIE

by L. DU GARDE PEACH, M.A., Ph.D., D.Litt.

with illustrations by F. HAMPSON

Publishers: Ladybird Books Ltd . Loughborough
© Ladybird Books Ltd (formerly Wills & Hepworth Ltd) 1970
Printed in England

MADAME CURIE

In the year 1867, in the city of Warsaw in Poland, a little girl was born who was to become one of the most famous women in the world. She was christened Manya, and her father and mother, who were Polish, were named Sklodovska.

Manya Sklodovska would be a very difficult name to remember. Fortunately, when later on Manya went to France and married a Frenchman, she became Madame Curie, a name which is today honoured in every civilised country.

Manya's father was a teacher of science, and one of her earliest memories was of a glass case full of bottles and scientific instruments. She had no idea what they were for, but they fascinated her.

Although Manya's parents were not rich, Manya grew up in a house where there were plenty of books. One day, when she was only four years old, she heard her elder sister Bronya stumbling over the reading aloud of a simple lesson. Manya reached out and, taking the book from her, read the passage without any mistakes. Suddenly she realised that her parents were staring at her in amazement. Little Manya started to cry. "I'm sorry," she said, "I didn't do it on purpose, but it's so easy."

Manya read the passage without any mistakes.

0 7214 0237 2

Soon Manya had to go to school. Here, too, she found everything easy. She had a wonderful memory and never forgot anything she had once read. Although two years younger than anyone else, she was always top of the class.

Life in Poland at that time was very difficult. Then the country was occupied by Czarist Russia, and the people of Poland had no freedom. Although Manya and all the other Polish children were supposed to do all their lessons in Russian, the teachers used the Polish language when the harsh Russian inspectors were not present. These inspectors used to come unexpectedly and ask the children questions about Russian history. It was always Manya who was brought out to answer them.

When she was sixteen, Manya finished her schooldays. She had won the highest award, a gold medal. Manya had been working very hard, and her father decided that she must have a year's holiday. Fortunately her father and mother had many relations who were farmers or small landowners. Manya's holiday was spent staying with her Uncle Xavier, who had fifty thoroughbred horses, or with her Uncle Zdzislav and his three jolly daughters.

Manya was always the one who answered the Inspector's questions.

Once in the country, Manya decided to forget all about things like physics and mathematics, at which she had been working so hard. She wrote to a friend: "I can't believe that geometry or algebra ever existed." For the first time in her life, Manya was enjoying utterly care-free idleness.

Amongst the excitements of her year in the country was one which she always remembered: the Kulig. This was a sort of fancy-dress dance, not in one place, but all over the country-side. Manya and her three cousins would dress up as Cracow peasant girls, and drive for miles over the frozen snow in sleighs, the bells on the horses' harness jingling happily as they galloped along. Other sleighs joined them, together with young men on horseback, in picturesque costumes, brandishing flaming torches.

All through the night they would drive, stopping to dance at one house after another. The sun rose and set, and still they drove and danced another night away. "You can't imagine how delightful it is!" Manya wrote.

The year of holiday finished with eight weeks for Manya and her younger sister Hela at the country house of the Countess de Fleury. Here Manya had her first experience of a very different kind of life.

8   *The care-free excitement of the Kulig.*

The eight weeks of garden parties, boating trips and dances – at one of which Manya danced right through the soles of a new pair of shoes – came to an end. Conditions at home now made it necessary for Manya to earn her living.

The only way which seemed possible was to take up teaching, and soon Manya was trudging the streets of Warsaw in all weathers, giving private lessons to the children of the rich. It was poor work for a brilliant pupil who would one day be recognised as a genius.

Although it was by teaching that she earned a little money, this was only a part of Manya's life. For many years the Russians had been trying to stamp out everything Polish, its language, its history – even its art. The result was an underground movement of thousands of young people determined to free their country from its rulers.

These young people were of all kinds. Some believed in violence and the throwing of bombs. Others, like Manya, devoted their time to learning and teaching the forbidden subjects. This had to be done secretly. If they had been discovered, they would all have been sent to prison.

10   *Manya trudged the streets of Warsaw.*

Manya had an elder sister, Bronya, whose one desire was to study at the medical school of the University, and to become a doctor. But in Warsaw the University did not admit women. To get a medical degree it was necessary to go to Paris. The big problem was that Bronya had insufficient money.

All her life Manya was always ready to sacrifice herself for others. She now suggested that she should become a governess in some rich family and, out of her wages, pay for Bronya to live in Paris. At first Bronya objected, but finally she agreed.

To help her sister financially, Manya became a governess in a place named Szczuki, near Przasnysz. The people were pleasant, and for three years Manya remained, working hard and sending money to her sister.

At the same time Manya did not forget her wish to do something for Poland and against her country's occupiers. Secretly she gathered together the children of the neighbouring peasants and taught them Polish songs, and stories from the history of their native land. She did this although she knew that if the Czar's police found out, she would be harshly punished.

Polish children learned their national songs and stories from Manya.

Although Manya worked long hours as a governess, and spent much of her leisure teaching the little Polish children, she still found time to continue her studies. Often she could be found, long after midnight, reading books on physics and mathematics.

All this time what she most wanted, and most lacked, was somewhere where she could actually do experiments in chemistry or physics. When she returned to Warsaw she found such a place; it was a very small laboratory, without all the complicated apparatus to be found in a real laboratory. It had in fact been organised by Manya's cousin as part of the secret education of the young people of Poland, whom the Russians of that time were determined to keep in ignorance. It was while working with this simple equipment that Manya suddenly realised what her life's work was to be. As she says, her vocation "flashed into life".

After a year of teaching in Warsaw, she had saved enough money to get to Paris to join Bronya. All she could afford was a fourth-class ticket, which meant spending some time travelling in an open van with only her luggage to sit on, and only such food as she had brought with her. Manya was not worried. She was determined to get to Paris.

Manya arriving in Paris.

In Paris, Manya breathed the air of a free country for the first time in her life. Here the people spoke their thoughts freely. Only someone brought up in a country under a foreign dictatorship could know what this meant to the Polish girl who stood enraptured on the steps of the French railway station.

Manya Sklodovska was not the sort of person to remain bewildered for very long. She had saved, rouble by rouble, the money to study at the Sorbonne, the name by which the University of Paris was known. Now the dream had come true. The great building of the Sorbonne was before her, and on a white poster were the words:

"Faculty of Science
Courses will begin at the Sorbonne on
November 3, 1891."

Manya, who now changed her name to the French equivalent, Marie, went to the first classes full of eager enthusiasm. She was quickly disappointed. She found that she did not speak French well enough to understand what the professor was saying. In addition, all her reading of physics and mathematics was of very little help. Poor Manya cried with vexation. It seemed as though all her sacrifices had been for nothing.

In Paris Manya breathed the air of a free country for the first time in her life.

Mademoiselle Marie Sklodovska, as she was now known, was not to be defeated by difficulties. She set to work to learn French thoroughly, and to catch up on her scientific studies.

At first Marie stayed with her sister Bronya, but soon she found that in order to work it was more convenient to live alone. She was very poor. All she could afford was an attic in which she had to do her own cooking on a little oil stove. There was no water, no heating and no light, except a skylight in the sloping roof.

When she had paid the rent, Marie had three francs a day on which to live, less than three shillings. Out of this she had to buy food and clothing. A new pair of shoes meant half-starving for weeks, and the two dresses which she had brought from Poland grew shabbier and shabbier.

Marie knew nothing about housekeeping. She could not even make soup, and for weeks she would live on bread and butter and tea. Often she could not afford coal for the little stove, and she would go on working until her hands were too cold to hold a pen. One day Marie fainted from cold and hunger.

18   *Alone in her attic, Marie fainted from cold and hunger.*

When Bronya's husband, Casimir, who was a doctor, heard what had happened, he at once brought Marie back to their flat and fed and doctored her. But Marie was too independent and too determined to work, and would not stay to be looked after. A week later she was back in her attic. The examinations were soon to be held, and she had to be ready for them.

If the character of this young woman could be put into four words, they would be 'patient', 'stubborn', 'determined' and 'systematic'. She had a passion for working in a laboratory. Everything down to the smallest detail in any experiment had to be checked and checked again before she was satisfied.

The examinations were held. Marie, again half-starved and her health undermined by hours of work in her unheated attic, saw the words on the examination paper dancing before her eyes.

She pulled herself together, and when the results were read out, the name of Marie Sklodovska was at the top of the list. Her first thought was to get back to Poland. For three months Marie rested and, what was more important, ate her way back to health. She was determined to return to Paris for more study.

Marie back in her attic, working for the examinations.

The difficulty, as always, was money. Then, unexpectedly, Marie was granted a scholarship for deserving students who wished to study abroad. It was for six hundred roubles, enough for Marie to live on for fifteen months.

She was now a very attractive young woman of twenty-six with a passion for work. The complicated apparatus in the physics laboratory meant more to Marie than all the young men at the Sorbonne who admired her. Then, quite suddenly, she fell in love.

Pierre Curie was thirty-five. He was also recognised as a physicist of genius. In the young Polish girl who had already passed brilliantly in her first examinations, he recognised a genius equal to his own. In July, 1895, Manya Sklodovska became Madame Pierre Curie.

Her entire wardrobe consisted of the two old shabby dresses which she had brought from Poland: she had nothing remotely resembling a wedding dress. When Casimir's mother offered to buy her a dress, she said, "If you are going to give me one, please let it be practical and dark, so that I can wear it afterwards to go to the laboratory." It was characteristic of her. All through her life her work came first. How many girls would have foregone the usual white wedding dress for such a reason?

22

Marie was very happy in her marriage. Pierre Curie was as devoted to scientific work as she was, and together they spent long hours in the laboratory. By the time she was thirty, Marie had taken two degrees.

However, it was to be years before she achieved the world-wide recognition which was to be hers. In the meantime life was not easy for M. and Mme. Curie.

In order to obtain the degree of Doctor of Science, it is necessary to write what is called a thesis. This is really a very long essay on some scientific subject, usually about some research or discovery made by the writer.

A French scientist named Becquerel had noticed that any solid matter which contained an element called uranium, gave off rays similar to X-rays. Nobody knew the cause of these rays, and Mme. Curie decided to try to find out. It was a slow and very complicated process, and in the middle of it Mme. Curie made a surprising discovery. A mineral called pitchblende was known to contain uranium and to give off these rays. Mme. Curie found that pitchblende produced a greater volume of radiation than could be accounted for by the amount of uranium which it contained.

Pierre and Marie spent long hours working together in the laboratory.

Curiosity is the first virtue of a scientist. Here was a mystery which could only be accounted for in one way: the pitchblende must contain something besides uranium, something which was even more radioactive.

In conditions which would have discouraged anyone less determined, Mme. Curie checked and re-checked her calculations. She had no properly equipped laboratory in which to work. All that was available was a dilapidated store-room at the School of Physics. It was cold, damp, and with no comfort whatsoever. What was worse, it had no proper electrical equipment, and none of the apparatus necessary for complicated experiments. In these almost impossible surroundings Mme. Curie did work which resulted in one of the greatest discoveries of the century.

However, life for her was not *all* work. Marie Curie loved the country. She and her husband now and then got out their bicycles and rode along the open roads of France. They lunched by the roadside on bread and cheese and fruit, and stayed the night at little wayside inns in unknown villages. The simple innkeepers did not suspect that this homely young couple, one of whom was a foreigner, sitting in the chimney corner by candlelight, were talking of things which were to change the world.

Pierre and Marie explored the countryside of France.

Ancient philosophers had wrongly thought that earth, air, fire and water were elements. An element is something which exists in a pure state and cannot be split into anything else. Gold and lead, and even gases are elements.

It was in the reign of Charles II that men became much more interested in science. King Charles himself founded the Royal Society to study subjects like physics, chemistry and mathematics. Soon a long list of elements had been compiled.

In their scientific work, Mme. Curie and her husband were looking for a previously unknown element – an element unlike any other.

In 1898, three years after she was married, Mme. Curie published, in a scientific paper, an article in which she suggested that there must be a new element combined in pitchblende, an element with very powerful radio-activity. She was determined, with the help of her husband, to find it. But first they had to obtain the pitchblende. Soon tons of what looked like dirty brown earth were being tipped at the door of the cold, leaking shed in which they worked.

Pitchblende being delivered to Marie outside the shed in which she and Pierre worked.

It was already known that pitchblende consisted of a number of different elements. What Mme. Curie now had to do was to extract from some tons of pitchblende all the elements known to be in it. What was left would be the new unknown element.

The question was – how much of this new element could be obtained from a hundred grammes of pitchblende? Mme. Curie thought that she might get about one gramme; actually she was to find that it required a million grammes of pitchblende to produce one gramme of the new element, radium.

Fortunately she did not know this. Not that it would have deterred her. Mme. Curie was not the sort of woman to be afraid of hard work or difficulties. She wrote later: "In this miserable old shed I sometimes passed the whole day stirring a boiling mass with an iron rod nearly as big as myself. In the evening I was broken with fatigue."

The physicists and chemists who read Mme. Curie's article were very doubtful. A new radioactive element would upset all their previous ideas. "Show us some radium," they said, "and we will believe you." Pierre and Marie were to work for four years to convince them.

A weary Marie stirred the pitchblende for whole days at a time.

The difficulties were tremendous. The air in the old shed was full of floating specks of coal-dust, which became mixed with the carefully purified chemical compounds. But nothing daunted Mme. Curie.

The days of work became months and years. In the summer the heat in the shed became almost unbearable; in the winter Marie and Pierre had to make cups of tea to keep a little heat in their bodies. It was a hard life, but with the prospect of a great discovery before them they scorned fatigues and difficulties.

The piles of pitchblende grew smaller. After each processing the little heap of purified pitchblende also became smaller, as more and more of the known elements were eliminated. Then, in 1902, Pierre and Marie Curie looked at a tiny speck of matter in a glass container.

That evening, as they sat in their poorly furnished flat, they suddenly felt that they must go to the old hut and look again at the result of so much work. As they opened the door, it squeaked as it had done for years. They stepped into the dark laboratory. "Don't light the lamps," said Marie. "Look!" There on the table, glowing in the darkness, was a tiny speck of blue-ish light. It came from pure radium.

The pure radium glowed in the darkness.

It had been a hard life for M. and Mme. Curie. With no grant for research, and only a miserable and unhealthy hut in which to work, they had been obliged to spend valuable time earning money by teaching at the School of Physics.

If anyone in authority in France had been able to realise the importance of the work which Pierre and Marie Curie were doing, M. Curie would have been made a professor and given an efficient laboratory. But little was done, except to offer Pierre the Cross of the Legion of Honour. Pierre Curie replied, "I do not feel the slightest need of being decorated, but I am in the greatest need of a laboratory."

Not only were they overworked – they did not allow themselves enough to eat. A friend wrote that he would often see Mme. Curie nibble two slices of sausage and swallow a cup of tea as she stood watching an experiment. This was often all she would have for her evening meal. It was not enough.

The University of Geneva in Switzerland was quick to recognise the importance of the discovery of radium. M. Curie was offered a professorship, with an "official position" for Mme. Curie. The offer was refused.

Even the need for a meal was not allowed to interfere with Pierre and Marie's work.

Nothing mattered to Pierre and Marie Curie except their research work on radium. Going to Switzerland would have meant neglecting it. They had suffered cold, hunger and poverty because of it; they were not going to desert it now.

As the work proceeded, their difficulties were increased by the action of radium itself. The radiation from uranium which had first attracted their attention, was comparatively harmless. But the radiation from radium was two million times stronger than that of uranium. Soon not only everything in the shed became radioactive, but blisters and sores appeared on their hands and did not heal for months.

One day their friend, Professor Becquerel, was carrying a small glass tube of radium in the pocket of his waistcoat. To his surprise he found that it had burned his skin through the glass tube and through his clothes. He hurried to tell M. and Mme. Curie what had happened.

Suddenly they realised that radium might be useful. If it could burn healthy skin, it might destroy diseased skin. It might even destroy cancer. In that moment it became clear that in discovering radium, Pierre and Marie Curie had made one of the most important contributions to medicine for a hundred years.

36 *Blisters and sores appeared on Pierre's and Marie's hands.*

Marie Curie had again and again put off her examination for the Degree of Doctor of Science. She was determined to be absolutely sure before she presented her thesis. Now she *was* sure.

The conferring of such a Degree was a very ceremonious occasion. The examiners, all distinguished men in full evening dress, sat behind a table. A large audience, equally distinguished, was also present to hear the candidates answer questions from the examiners.

Marie Curie cared nothing for ceremony. Left to herself, she would have gone to the examination in her old dress. It was her sister, Bronya, who made her do something which she had not done for a long time: buy a new dress.

Like her wedding dress, it had to be one which she could afterwards wear in the laboratory. So we can picture this young Polish woman of thirty-six, the discoverer of radium, standing in a simple, dark dress, confidently facing her examiners. She answered every question without hesitation, sometimes writing a complicated formula on a blackboard. The technical expressions meant nothing to the general audience, but in her monotonous, quietly-spoken sentences, the scientists present realised that they were hearing something which must change all their ideas of the universe.

The scientists realised that they had to change their ideas of the universe.

Pierre and Marie Curie had discovered how to isolate pure radium. No-one else could do it. It was their secret. It was also a very valuable secret. If Marie Curie was right in thinking that radium could cure cancer, the demand for it would be world-wide. Already an American firm had written to M. Curie, asking for details of the process. Other firms were sure to follow, and all were ready to pay large sums of money for the information. If M. and Mme. Curie were to patent their method of producing radium, they could be millionaires in a year.

Pierre and Marie looked at one another and smiled. To anyone who did not think as they did, the temptation would have been irresistible.

"It is impossible," said Marie. Pierre sighed. "We could have a fine laboratory," he said. Marie shook her head. "It would be contrary to the scientific spirit," she said. There was no further argument. They had made their choice between riches and comparative poverty – between what they believed to be their duty as scientists, and wealth beyond their wildest dreams. Without giving it another thought, they mounted their bicycles and rode off into the woods. They came back that evening tired but happy, their arms full of flowers.

Pierre and Marie gathered wild flowers.

Pierre and Marie could cheerfully give up a fortune, but they could not avoid becoming two of the most famous people in the world. The first honour came from London, when M. Curie was invited to lecture at the Royal Institute, and Mme. Curie was the first woman ever to be present at one of its meetings.

All London wanted to see the discoverers of radium. They were invited to parties and banquets where Marie, in her simple dark dress, was surrounded by women wearing expensive gowns and magnificent jewels, and Pierre in a shabby dress suit seemed to find it difficult to believe that the compliments were addressed to himself and his wife.

They shared the famous Nobel Prize with their friend, Henri Becquerel, but were not present to receive it. They let their little daughter play with gold medals which they received from various distinguished societies.

Personal fame was disliked by Mme. Curie. Once a reporter, who had been sent to interview her, found her sitting on the steps of a fisherman's cottage, shaking the sand out of her shoes. When he asked her questions about herself, she replied with a sentence which summed up her life: "In science we must be interested in things, not in persons."

All London wanted to see the discoverers of radium.

In 1906 Pierre Curie was killed in a road accident. This was not only a most terrible tragedy for his wife, but also a very great loss to science. Although it was Mme. Curie who had first established the existence of the new element radium, Pierre had worked with her on the long task of separating out pure radium.

With immense courage Mme. Curie did not allow her personal sorrow to interfere with her work. Work became the one thing remaining for which to live. Fortunately she was no longer poor. She had been appointed to the professorship held by Pierre, the first woman in France to hold such a position.

Mme. Curie's devotion to science was only equalled by her lack of interest in money or fame. After many long years of work, she had one gramme of radium. It was calculated to be worth a million gold francs. She gave it to the University without a second thought.

In 1910, she refused the award of the Legion of Honour, but in the following year she was awarded – and accepted – the Nobel Prize. When the King of Sweden personally presented the Diploma to Mme. Curie, she became the only person ever to receive this world-famous award for the second time.

The death of Pierre in an accident.

There were many people in France who were bitterly jealous of Mme. Curie. She was attacked in the press and openly insulted by these mean and despicable persons. She became ill, and later an operation was necessary. Her convalescence was passed on the coast of England, in the peaceful home of an English friend.

At this moment when to Mme. Curie, physically and mentally depressed, the future seemed black, a deputation arrived from Poland. It was proposed to set up a Radium Institute in Warsaw, and Mme. Sklodovska Curie was invited to become its Director.

She had to refuse, much as she would have loved to return to her native city. A fine Radium Institute was being built in Paris, and she felt that it was her duty to remain in charge of it. However, she attended the opening of the Institute in Warsaw, where she had the great joy of delivering the first lecture; it was in the language forbidden in her youth – the language of Poland.

Occupied as she was with the building of the Paris Radium Institute in the Rue Pierre Curie, a street named after her husband, she found time to come to England to receive from Birmingham University an academic degree.

Marie received an academic degree from Birmingham University.

Then suddenly, in the summer of 1914, France was at war. Paris was threatened by the German Army, and Mme. Curie's first thought was for the precious gramme of radium. Frail and suffering as she was, she packed it in a heavy lead container and boarded a crowded train for Bordeaux.

On the journey to Bordeaux she was unnoticed amongst the crowd of civilians fleeing from Paris, but once the gramme of radium was safe in a Bordeaux bank, she decided to return. She was the only civilian on a troop-train full of soldiers.

Back in Paris she found that the doctors of the army were very short of X-ray units. X-rays make it possible to photograph bullets or shell fragments inside the body of a wounded man. This is a great help to the surgeon.

Soldiers do not like civilians, especially women, to interfere in their arrangements. Mme. Curie was still weak from her illness, but like Florence Nightingale – about whom you may read in another Ladybird book – she overcame all opposition. She organised a fleet of mobile X-ray vans, one of which she even drove herself. Thanks to her, more than a million wounded soldiers benefited from the "Little Curies" – the name by which the X-ray vans were known.

Marie driving a mobile X-ray van.

The war over, Mme. Curie found that she had to face the fatigue and, to her, the embarrassment of world fame. In America all the cities and universities invited her. Honorary degrees were bestowed upon her: civic welcomes were organised by the score: she was presented with the Freedom of the City of New York.

The women of America subscribed a hundred thousand dollars for a gramme of radium, which was presented to her by the President of the United States at the White House. She gave it to the Radium Institute in Paris.

Her simplicity and complete disregard for money or honours puzzled the Americans, but it also won their admiration and affection. On a second visit Mme. Curie was presented with another gramme of radium, which she immediately gave to the Radium Institute in Warsaw.

Mme. Curie had received the Nobel Prize twice, six other distinguished prizes, seventeen honorary doctorates, and honorary membership of more than eighty scientific societies all over the world. Now at last France paid its debt by giving her a pension of forty thousand francs. In 1927, threatened by blindness, she wrote: "I do not know whether I could live without the laboratory". It had seen her life's work in the service of humanity.

Marie was welcomed in America.

Series 708
Lives of the Great Scientists